Mahatma Gandhi on Sarvodaya

Also Available:

- — Mahatama Gandhi on Ethics
- — Mahatma Gandhi on Sarvodaya
- — Revisiting Hind Swaraj
- — Mahatma Gandhi on Untouchability
- — Understanding Gandhi

About the Author

Dr. Anil Dutta Mishra is a distinguished Gandhian scholar and writer. He started his career as Assistant Professor in the Department of Non-violence and Peace Studies, Jain Vishva Bharati University, Ladnun, Rajasthan, became Deputy Director of National Gandhi Museum and Honorary Professor, Centre for Gandhian Philosophy and Human Development, Gayatri Vidya Parishad Degree College [Autonomous], Visakhapatnam.

Dr. Mishra has held the post of General Secretary of Indian Society of Gandhian Studies, Alliance for Sarvodaya, Member Board of Studies, Nagpur and Panjab Universities and is Member of Gandhian Studies Centre of different colleges and universities across India sponsored by UGC and Executive Member IIPA Regional Branch. He has authored/edited 30 books and published a number of research papers. His recent book **Reading Gandhi** is widely acclaimed.
Email: anilduttamishra@gmail.com

MAHATMA GANDHI ON SARVODAYA

Anil Dutta Mishra

CONCEPT PUBLISHING COMPANY PVT. LTD.
NEW DELHI-110059

ISBN-13 : 978-93-5125-120-0

First Published 2015

Published and Printed by

Concept Publishing Company Pvt. Ltd.
A/15-16, Commercial Block, Mohan Garden
New Delhi-110059 (India)
T: 25351460, 25351794, *F*: 091-11-25357109
E: publishing@conceptpub.com, W: www.conceptpub.com
Editorial Office: H-13, Bali Nagar, New Delhi-110 015, India.

Cataloging in Publication Data—*Courtesy:* D.K. Agencies (P) Ltd. <docinfo@dkagencies.com>

Mishra, Anil Dutta, 1965-
Mahatma Gandhi on sarvodaya / Anil Dutta Mishra.
p. cm.
Includes bibliographical references and index.
ISBN 9789351251200

1. Gandhi, Mahatma, 1869-1948—Political and social views. 2. Sarvodaya movement--India. I. Title.

DDC 303.4840954 23

Preface

"Mahatma Gandhi on Sarvodaya" is the fifth volume of the series containing Gandhi's original writings and speeches. The purpose of this book is to revisit Gandhi. The fact is that the entire world is in grip of violence of various types; there is a moral bankruptcy; accountability, ethics, honesty and governance are at the receiving end; there is economy meltdown and growth has gone down in the developed as well as the developing countries. Capitalism and Marxism both have miserably failed to solve the human miseries. Liberalisation, privatisation and globalization have encouraged chronic capitalism. The result is unrest and violence everywhere. In India Maosim/Naxalism is spreading its wings even in the urban areas. The structural violence/invisible violence is also on the increase. Immorality and corruption is no longer a social taboo rather it has become a matter of pride for the individuals. The so-called Gandhians and the Gandhian Institutions are also not immune from *Kanchan* and *Kamini*. Immorality is taught in the name of morality by Gandhians and its institutions. Therefore, it is essential to revisit Gandhi's core ideas and position it in the contemporary context. Sarvodaya is one of the essential ideas of Gandhi. In 1908, Gandhi abridged Ruskin's *Unto This Last* under the title "*Sarvodaya*" and published in an eight-part series.

Gandhi was responding to the challenges he was confronting. His concern was towards the immediate problems but his response was timeless. *Sarvodaya* is one of the alternative to capitalism and socialism. It is a non-violent socio-economic and political order. Gandhi himself rightly said on July 21, 1938 at Seaon—*"Sarvodaya is impossible without satyagraha. The word satyagraha should be understood here in its etymological sense. There can be no insistence on truth where there is no non-violence. Hence the attainment of sarvodaya depends upon the attainment of non-violence. The attainment of non-violence in its turn depends upon tapascharya. Tapascharya, again, should be pure. Ceaseless effort, discretion, etc., should form part of it. Pure tapascharya leads to pure knowledge. Experience shows that although people talk of non-violence, many are mentally so lazy that they do not even take the trouble of familiarizing themselves with the facts. Take an example. India is a poor country. We wish to do away with poverty. But how many people have made a study of how this poverty came about, what its implications are, how it can be removed, etc.? A devotee of non-violence, should be full of such knowledge. It is the duty of Sarvodaya to create such means and not to enter into controversies. Editors of Sarvodaya should forget Gandhism. There is no such thing as Gandhism. I have not put anything new before India; I have only presented an ancient thing in a new way. I have tried to utilize it in a new field. Hence, my ideas cannot be appropriately called Gandhism. We shall adopt truth wherever we find it, praise it wherever we see it, and pursue it. In other words, in every sentence of Sarvodaya, we should catch a glimpse of non-violence and knowledge."*

In this introductory background, an attempt has been made to put his writings on *Sarvodaya* at one place for proper understanding of the philosophy of *Sarvodaya* using only primary source. To make the book reader friendly, it has been divided into two parts. In Part One, an attempt has been made to present a broader philosophy of *Sarvodaya* keeping all the contemporary discourses and challenges in mind. In Part Two, Gandhi's original writings on *Sarvodaya* is placed for reader's deeper understanding of the subject.

In writing this book I had received, over the years, very valuable help from friends, teachers and colleagues. I am grateful to them. My family has always stood behind me in all my academic endeavours. My wife, Dr. Sweta Mishra, Associate Professor, Department of Political Science, Gargi College, University of Delhi, went through the final draft and provided her valuable inputs.

Last but not the least, I am grateful to Shri Ashok Kumar Mittal of Concept Publishing Company Pvt. Ltd., for bringing out this book in present form and that too within record time.

21st May, 2014

Anil Dutta Mishra

anilduttamishra@gmail.com

Contents

Part Two
Gandhi on Sarvodaya

PART ONE
INTRODUCTION
[Sarvodaya: Beyond Capitalism and Marxism]

1

Introduction

[Sarvodaya: Beyond Capitalism and Marxism]

Sarvodaya, today, does not represent a mere vision or utopian notion but makes an attempt of reorienting human mind to reconstruct human society. It has assumed the dimensions of a movement and a socio-economic force of great potentialities. It is a dynamic philosophy, which can make possible the advent of a radically transformed humanity. Sarvodaya seeks to build a new society on the foundations of old spiritual and moral values of India and attempts to meet the challenge of the contemporary problems.[1] The world has witnessed the propagation, experimentation and implementation of various socio-economic ideologies – capitalist, socialist and communist, time to time. But, in overall consideration, Sarvodaya is undoubtedly far more superior to other attributive models. It envisages a well-balanced and integrated development of the nation with no distinction among have and have-nots, privileged and underprivileged, ruler and ruled. The essence of Sarvodaya though lies in socialising matter through the strength of the spirit. Dogmas have no place in Sarvodaya. "The philosophy of Sarvodaya is not a set of dogmas, in its essence, it is compatible with an attempt of the spirit to prevail over matter and to socialise itself."[2] Sarvodaya is a redeemer's philosophy of social and political orientation, where suffering is, Sarvodaya goes to mitigate it. It is the culmination of human emotional integration and the highest intellectual aspiration. It is a symbol of platonic detachment and Gita's Anasakti.[3] It is the highest manifestation of love and attempts at a mental transformation of the people. Gandhi denounced the utilitarian principle of the greatest good of the greatest number, and advocated the sarvodaya philosophy.

Gandhi did not originally coin the word " Sarvodaya". Even before him, the idea of sarvodaya was found in religious books: *Vedas*, *Upanishads*, *The Ramayan*, *The Gita*, *Quran* and many others. It was also preached by Indian and Western saints as well as philosophers. But Gandhi gave to these age-old principles and ideals an extended meaning and application. In fact, after the death of Gandhi, the word "Sarvodaya" came into greater prominence, when his fellow-workers assembled at Sevagram (Wardha), in March 1948, and decided to form an organization named 'Sarvodaya Samaj'. This name was chosen in preference to that of 'Satyagraha Mandal' (Satyagraha Circle) because the word 'Satyagraha' had come to acquire a restricted meaning which did not include constructive work. Since then the school of thought which accepts Gandhi's philosophy in all its aspects and of which the central figure is Vinoba Bhave, has come to be known as the 'Sarvodaya School' and its philosophy as the `Sarvodaya Philosophy'.[4] The prominent thinkers of this school were Acharya Vinoba Bhave, Kishorlal Ghanshyam Mashruwala, J.C. Kumarappa, Kaka Kalelkar, Shankerrao Deo, Dhirendra Mazumdar, Loknayak Jayaprakash Narayan and Acharya J.B. Kripalani. Except Jayaprakash Narayan, all of them had been associated with Gandhi in his constructive work.

Sarvodaya: Meaning and Genesis

'Sarvodaya' is Sanskrit in origin which comprised 'Sarva' meaning all and 'Udaya' meaning rising. The etymological meaning of sarvodaya is the rising of all. This 'all' includes all living beings.[5] In other words, sarvodaya as the word means welfare of all. The word first appeared in the form of the title for the Gujarati translation of John Raskin's book entitled '*Unto this Last*'.[6] Sarvodaya was the title of series of nine articles, which Gandhi wrote and got published in Gujarati in the *Indian Opinion* Weekly in South Africa in 1908.[7]

Sarvodaya is essentially a spiritual activity, which has two meanings, viz., negative and positive. As a negative concept, Sarvodaya is not limited to one person or to one group of persons. Nobody is excluded from enjoying anything from other.[8] It is not something which one man or set of men can gain or enjoy to the exclusion of others.[9] As a positive concept, Sarvodaya implies the participation of all kinds of people irrespective of class, caste, creed and religion. It also stands for the total blossoming of all the faculties – physical, mental and spiritual of the human being. It is an activity in which all may partake and if it is to amount to a full realization of the human faculties of the human soul.[10]

According to Acharya Vinoba Bhave, the term 'Sarvodaya' commands a two-fold meaning. Firstly, Sarvodaya means making all happy by removing suffering and poverty with the help of scientific knowledge. Secondly, establishing a world state full with divinity, kindness and equality is called Sarvodaya.[11] Sarvodaya aims not at the rise of the few or the many, or for that matter the rise of the greatest number. It is not utilitarianism, which stands for the greatest good of the greatest number. It contains the germ of minority and majority. Contrary to utilitarianism stands for the good of one and all, of the high and the low, of the strong and the weak, the intelligent as well as the dull. As against the *Laissez faire* theory, that is the survival of the fittest, Sarvodaya believes in the survival and development of all. To Vinoba, "The idea of

Sarvodaya, as preached by the *Gita* is to merge oneself in the good of all."[12]

Apart from connoting the welfare of all, Sarvodaya commands two more meanings, firstly, the universal welfare and secondly, the integrated development of all. The *laissez faire* philosophy stands for the exploitation of many by a few. The utilitarian school supports the majority, totally neglecting the minority. Sarvodaya rejects these theories, which stand for the joy of few, advocates the welfare of all, irrespective of class, caste, creed, colour, race, region or religion. The philosophy of Sarvodaya makes the attempt or reorienting human mind, of reconstructing human society. It means welfare and prosperity of all. All must progress together without collision of interest.[13] Interpreting the purport of Sarvodaya, Dada Dharmadhikari said: "Sarvodaya is a term with a wider connotation since it conceives of assimilation of all and not only of many or most.[14] Sarvodaya is a philosophy, which provides checks against the imperfections of human mind and soul.

As regards the meaning of the word "Sarvodaya", there are broadly two views: the first, in its micro-form, means simply the rise of one and all; and secondly, the macro-form connotes the rise of all, the universal welfare and the all-round development of all.[15] But it connotes several other meanings. In its negative sense, it never omits even a single person from enjoying anything from the rest of the mankind. As a positive concept, it promotes the development of all the faculties of man. According to Vinoba Bhave, it stands for not only making all happy by eliminating suffering from all but also for bringing a world state based on equality. For Gandhi, Sarvodaya as a broader concept stands for the merger of one in all with self-sacrifice and a selfless service. It aims at not only fulfilling the minimum material needs but also developing the ethico-spiritual aspects of all people.

Sources of Sarvodaya

The following sources helped Gandhi to develop his concept of Sarvodaya. These were - Ruskin's book *Unto This Last*, Tolstoy's *The Kingdom of God is Within You*, Thoreau's *Civil Disobedience*, The *Bhagvad Gita*, *Isavasyopanisad*, Buddhism, Jainism, and Islam.

Ruskin's *Unto This Last*

The Gandhian philosophy of Sarvodaya can be traced to the central teachings of India's spiritual and religious heritage although Gandhi admits the fact that he had immediate inspiration from Ruskin's *Unto This Last* of which the term Sarvodaya is his rendering.[16] The welfare of all became the basic idea of Gandhi's philosophy right from the days when he wrote in Gujarati his most world famous thirty thousand words book '*Hind Swaraj* or *Indian Home Rule*' in 1909.

Gandhi called one of the chapters of his Autobiography '*The Magic Spell of Book*' wherein he describes the effects of Ruskin's *Unto This Last* (meaning uplift of the last). He translated it later into Gujrati claiming it Sarvodaya. It is a book from which Gandhi drew great inspiration and he at once determined to change his view of life in line with the ideals embodied in Ruskin's book *Unto This Last.*[17]

The central teachings of *Unto This Last*, according to Gandhi are:

(i) That the good of the individual is contained in the good of all.

(ii) That a lawyer's work has the same values as the Barber's inasmuch as all have the same right of earning their livelihood from their work.

(iii) That a life of labour, i.e. the life of the tiller of the soil and the handicraftsman is the life worth living.

There is a controversy with regard to the meanings of the terms "Unto This Last" and "Sarvodaya". Gandhi himself acknowledged that he translated it later into Gujrati, entitling it Sarvodaya. On the one hand, Benudhar Pradhan opines that the idea of welfare of all formed a part of his mental make-up even before he read this book.[18] This view is further strengthened from what Gandhi has expressed in his own words— "The first of these I knew."[19] On the other hand, Geoffery Ashe doubted whether the idea of Sarvodaya is contained at all in Ruskin's *Unto This Last.* Persons like Benudhar affirms that "it will be a travesty of truth to say that the objective of 'welfare of all' does not remain couched in the pages of *Unto This Last* of Ruskin."[20]

Ruskin and Gandhi both, were earnestly concerned with social welfare. While Ruskin aimed at the social welfare of 'the greatest number', Gandhi aimed at the welfare of all. Therefore, Vinoba Bhave feels that Gandhi is the real author of the term Sarvodaya, since the term, 'Unto This Last' would mean only the uplift of the last (*Antyodaya*). In fact, one has to accept that Ruskin's '*Unto This Last*' had directly or indirectly a profound influence on Gandhi in fulfilling the ideal of Sarvodaya, which he had already cherished as his life's mission.

Leo Tolstoy's *The Kingdom of God is within You*

Gandhi was greatly influenced by Leo Tolstoy, through his book '*The Kingdom of God is within You*' and his essay on 'Christianity and Patriotism'. Tolstoy's simplicity of life and purity of purpose influenced Gandhi deeply. His views on Christianity, its church, its teachings roused Gandhi's feelings. Tolstoy accepted love to be the law of life. The principle of non-violence is based on love for the entire mankind. Tolstoy and Gandhi, both adopted the instrument of love to solve all problems in their lives. In his celebrated book *The Kingdom of God is within You*, we find a political force creating an indelible mark on Gandhi. Gandhi confessed that its reading cured him of the skepticism and made him a firm believer of *Ahimsa*. Both Tolstoy and Gandhi firmly believed that non-violence could cure all social maladies, remove political ills, and establish peace on the earth and goodwill among mankind. In fact, both Tolstoy and Gandhi believed in the efficacy of love for the cure of evil and suffering in this world. Tolstoy perceived the truth, love and non-violence and Gandhi grasped the essence of these virtues and led his life directed towards these paths.[21]

Tolstoy also impressed upon Gandhi's mind the importance of bread-labour. For Tolstoy, the man who abstains from manual labour is a thief of the society. Gandhi acknowledged his debt to Tolstoy. He says, 'the law that to live man must work, first come home to me upon reading Tolstoy's writing, '*On Bread Labour*'—only those man deserve to eat bread who actually till the ground, spin cloth and produce things'. Tolstoy says, 'let us get off the shoulder of our neighbours' and Gandhi adds that if everyone performed that simple operation, he would have rendered all service God requires of him. Since every man has an obligation to himself as well as to the society, bread labour becomes an imperative duty which must be performed by each and every man.[22]

Gandhian philosophy of Sarvodaya comes very close to Tolstoyan philosophy of anarchism. The pure ideal of Gandhi's conception of Sarvodaya is an ideal of philosophical anarchism, a stateless society marked by voluntary co-operation. Profound faith in God, commiseration from the exploited, inherent aversion to violence, deep-rooted belief in the dignity of man led the two philosophers to the same goal and objective. But Gandhi is not a through-going Tolstoyan. The difference between the two philosophers arises out of the fact that Gandhi is far more practical than Tolstoy. Tolstoy recoils from all expressions of violence. Gandhi permits violence, provided of course, that motive for violence is not anger but true love. Thus, the moral content of Gandhi's doctrine of *Ahimsa*, which forms the fulcrum around which the entire doctrine of Sarvodaya ideology is based, has a higher significance than that of Tolstoy's. This is due to the fact that Gandhi was greatly influenced by the *Gita* ideal of *niskamakarma*, i.e. action without attachment.[23]

Thoreau's *Civil Disobedience*

The American pacifist Thoreau was the champion of the free sprit and was repelled by the established political and economic routine of time. In him we discover an element of moral individualism culminating in his concept of 'civil disobedience'. Thoreau used the term in his speeches in 1849. It is obvious that Gandhi did not derive his idea of 'civil disobedience' from the writings of Thoreau. In fact, the resistance to authority in South Africa preceded before Gandhi got the essay of Thoreau on 'Civil Disobedience'. This movement was then known as 'passive resistance'. Gandhi was not satisfied with the term 'civil disobedience' because it failed to convey the full meaning of the struggle. Hence, he adopted the phrase 'civil resistance'.[24]

Thoreau did not believe in narrow sectarianism and felt that man is meant to experience God, not to theologies about him. Man according to Thoreau is a social being who is generally disposed to co-operation with fellow beings for social good. He felt that the moral institutions of the state supported by coercive authority hamper the individual's moral and spiritual freedom. He, therefore, visualised a society in which government will disappear. 'That Government is best which governs not at all', or, 'which governs least'. Like Thoreau, Gandhi also held that the democracy could be realized only in a stabiles society based on Truth and Non-violence. And Gandhi described it as Sarvodaya, which promotes not only social welfare but spiritual upliftment. Thus, Gandhi heard an echo of his own thought in Thoreau.[25]

The Bhagvad Gita

Gandhi drew his primary strength and inspiration from the *Bhagvad Gita.* To Gandhi, the *Gita* is the 'Eternal Mother'. According to him, the theme of *Gita* is self-realization. He says: "self-realization and its means is the theme of the *Gita*".[26] Again he affirms, "to one who reads the spirit of the *Gita*, it teaches the secret of non-violence the secret of realizing the self through the physical body."[27]

The sole aim of the *Gita* is to suppress unrighteousness and to establish *Dharma.* It wants to bring prosperity and peace to all. It presents in concise form the Hindu view of life, which in turn stands for the universal brotherhood of all beings. It also highlights the importance of all selfless service for the promotion of the welfare of the whole creation since God and the creation is one. Through *Svadharma*, the *Gita* aims at '*Sarvabhutahita*' or the good of all beings.[28] In this way, *Gita* preaches the message of the welfare of all or Sarvodaya, which influenced Gandhi's thought, and action.

Isavasyopanisad

The first verse of Isavasyopanisad deals with the ideology of Sarvodaya. The first part of the verse contains the principles of equality and fraternity. And the second part reveals the ideas of renunciation, non-acquisitiveness, non-exploitation and service to the society. According to Gandhi, since the entire universe is pervaded by God, the verse preaches the philosophy of equality and fraternity, which are the fundamental principles of the welfare of all. He confirms, "Universal brotherhood not only brotherhood of all human beings but of all living beings, I find in this mantra..."[29]

Buddhism

According to Lord Buddha, all life is suffering. Suffering has to be extirpated in order to enjoy the bliss of *Nirvana*, which is the highest goal in Buddhism. *Nirvana* is both individualistic and universal or cosmic. It may be realized in his life, here and there. It may also be known as full and perfect enlightenment for the sake of all beings. All can obtain *nirvana* if they meticulously follow the Noble Eight-Fold Path of Buddha. Gandhi was highly influenced and deeply impressed by the Buddhist philosophy, which preached universal love, non-injury to living beings, sacrifice and renunciation for the sake of promoting the welfare of all. The Buddha stressed on purity of means, which in turn influenced Gandhi who constantly maintained that there is indissoluble relationship between pure means and noble end.[30] Buddha preached about the middle path. Similarly, in Sarvodaya, it is understood that no one should take extreme step.

Jainism

The ideal of the welfare of all forms is the cornerstone of the Jainism. *Ahimsa* forms one of the five vows. The positive aspect of non-violence is the love for fellow beings, not only human but also all creatures. A Jain Tirthankara's duty is to devote his whole life for showering happiness on all the beings of the whole universe. About the place of Sarvodaya in Jainism, Benudhar Pradhan states: "The concept of welfare of all was so much an integral part of Jaina philosophy that the term 'Sarvodaya' was used by one Jaina teacher Samantabhadra even before the Christian era."[31] Further, Benudhar Pradhan argues that though the word 'Sarvodaya' is used by the Jaina Saint Samantabhadra for the first time, yet Gandhi's use of the word is completely his own. According to him, the term Sarvodaya came to Gandhi "as if in a flash."[32] Therefore, he maintains that "the word Sarvodaya … was purely his own coinage."[33]

Islam

Gandhi had a great respect for Islam. He learnt the message of universal brotherhood from it. As for Islam, Gandhi declares that in his view, 'the point of brotherhood is manifested in no other religion as clearly as in Islam'. The reading of the holy Koran convinced Gandhi that the basis of Islam is not violence.[34] In fact, Gandhi shows remarkable catholicity and sympathetic and reverential attitude towards all religions of the world.

Apart from *Unto This Last, The Kingdom of God is within You*, the Upanishads, the *Gita*, Buddhism, and Jainism, Gandhia's concept of Sarvodaya was also influenced by Vaishnavism, Zoroastrianism and Christianity. The revival of the ancient teachings by Gandhi and incorporating them in his philosophy of Sarvodaya is perhaps his greatest contribution to the world of thought. Gandhi attempted the synthesis of the ideas of Vedanta, Buddhism, Jainism, Christianity and the teaching of prophets like Tulsidas, Tolstoy, Thoreau, Ruskin and national leaders of the Indian Renaissance movement. The philosophy of Sarvodaya takes up the Gandhian synthesis and tries to work out the implication of their ideas at more critical and analytical levels.[35]

Ends and Means in Sarvodaya

Morality is the essential means to achieve spirituality and good society or good ends. But communists like Machiavelli maintain that end justifies the means. This reveals that through any impure means like cunning, hypocrisy, hatred or violence one can get one's own desired end. To them, ends and means are watertight compartment. End is everything, no matter what or how the means are. Means become good if they serve the end. Jayaprakash Narayan observed impartially: "In Marxism any means are good means provided they serve the ends of the social revolution."[36]

For Gandhi means determine the end. He says, "As the means so the end".[37] Means are as important as the ends. In a way, his unique contribution to the world lies in his maintaining that the means are more important than the ends."[38] His emphasis on means rather than on the end is based on the doctrine of *niskamakarma* which holds that a person can have control over actions and not on their fruit. Gandhi is fully convinced that man can only strive but cannot command results. He maintains that "means are after all everything. There is no wall of separation between means and ends. Indeed the creator gives us control over means, none over the end. Realization of the goal is in exact proportion to that of the means. This is a proportion that admits of no exception."[39] Gandhi stress on the strength of the means is based on the following reasons: (i) He believes in the progressive evolution of man; (ii) He fixes the end of man as self-perfection; (iii) He feels that the end is always out of man's grip till it is attained; and (iv) He is convinced that if means are subordinated to ends, the ends to which means are subordinated are likely to be less effective. All the above conviction made Gandhi to held the view that man must have complete control over means, despite both means and ends are various and contradictory.[40]

According to Gandhi, the end justifying the means is dangerous in practice and unsound ethically. If it is accepted, it permits resource to violence, fraud, untruth, opportunism etc. Gandhi viewed human beings as supreme. They are ends in themselves. If the means are pure, the end also becomes pure. When we take care of the means, the end will take care of itself.[41] By emphasizing only the means, Gandhi does not intend to give a secondary place to the ends. To him, means and ends are inseparably connected just like seed and trees are connected.[42]

By considering means and ends as a continuous process, Gandhi dissolved the age-old opinion of viewing both as water-tight compartments. The difference between them is imaginary.[43] Therefore, he takes them as an organic whole. In a way, he proposes that both means and end must be homogeneous. He also holds that the extreme of means is itself the end. That is, the end progressively realizes itself through the means. The end can never result all of a sudden out of the means. In fact, when means slowly progresses, it turns itself into the end. The means apart from leading to an end shapes the end. In Gandhian philosophy, self-realization or spiritual freedom is the end of all human actions. Gandhi throughout his life tirelessly tried to use sarvodaya social order as the means to achieve spiritual freedom. Sarvodaya society guarantees moral freedom to every individual. This moral freedom, in turn, progresses itself into spiritual freedom, when it is followed meticulously placing faith in the supremacy of God. Moral freedom as means and spiritual freedom as end forms a continuous process or organic wholes. They cannot be divided into watertight compartments. Their difference is only imaginary. Both are convertible terms. That is what Gandhi too reveals. What is needed is understanding and practicing ethics as god has given. Sarvodaya, as it enjoys ethico-spiritual basis, it can also be equitable both moral freedom and spiritual freedom. Thus, the problem of ends and means, as an organic whole, occupies a unique place in Gandhian thought, contributing to sarvodaya, moral freedom, spiritual freedom, political freedom, and spiritual economic freedom.

Sarvodaya Social Order

Gandhi with his many-sided personality had a clear vision and definite approach to the problems, which faced India of his time. Indian society was full with deep-rooted evils. It had totally degenerated itself socially, politically, economically and educationally. Penury had further ruined Indian social conditions which were already corroded with caste-conflicts, child-marriages, untouchability, *Sati*, *Pardah*, negation of education to women, dowry, polygamy, corruption, exploitation, etc. Gandhi tried to find immediate solutions to all these problems.[44]

In sarvodaya society, there is no scope for exploitation, discrimination, inequality, and violence. Gandhi[45] envisaged that sarvodaya society should also be free from evils like 'politics without principle', 'wealth without work', 'knowledge without character', 'commerce without morals', 'science without mankind' and 'service without scarifices'. It should not be divided into watertight compartments called social, political and religious where all these act and react upon one another. His aim of sarvodaya made him to establish a close correlation among these problems. The sarvodaya society is an indivisible whole. In order to establish a democratic and free society Gandhi suggested every individual to imbibe the spirit of love, tolerance, kindness, fearlessness, non-violence etc. A non-violent society, however small it is, is the strongest one. Non-violence as the law of life includes individuals, societies and nations. To him, non-violence is both a personal and social virtue. A society built on the basis of complete *Ahimsa* is the purest anarchy.[46]

For Sarvodaya mentality, certain attributes are essential. Gandhi has offered the 'eleven vows' to discipline oneself so that a disciplined society could emerge. Self-scarifie is the essence of Sarvodaya Social Order. Every individual is to be ready and willing to sacrifice his happiness for the sake of others. Everyone is to follow the policy of giving and not taking. He is to work for others and not to expect anything in return for the same. Through Sarvodaya he wanted to rebuild the nation "from the bottom up-wards" and establish a new social order based on freedom, justice, equality and fraternity. Gandhi's ideal (Sarvodaya) society will be marked by following characteristics:[47]

- There should be no coercive state power in it and social cohesion should be maintained through the citizens' sense of social obligation like the obligations of *Varnashram Dharma* in ancient India.
- It should consist of villages or rural agricultural settlements in which wants are few and co-operation, conservation and decentralization are the governing norms of social, civil and economic activity.
- Besides agriculture, other production should be based on cottage industries and handicraft. Even education should be handicraft-centred.
- The ruling principles of decentralized and handicraft-centred production, three other economic norms should be maintained or practiced, namely village self-

sufficiency, bread-labour (i.e. winning one's bread through work done by one's own body labour), and non-possession (acquiring or using the minimum possible articles of consumption). Heavy machines and heavy transport will have no place in this society.

- In such a society, disputes or conflict (generally arising out of the craze for power, property or possession) will be few and for between. But in order to deal with such disputes, as may possibly or occasionally arise, village panchayats should be organised. In the unlikely event of the failure of panchayats, recourse may be had to *Satyagraha*.

Gandhi had set up his first sarvodaya community on a farm near Durban and called it Phoenix (c. 1904), followed by another one (c. 1910) over Johannesburg named after Leo Tolstoy. The idea behind these two settlements was that the inmates had to perform all chores of running the farms, whatever is their avocation, on living wages, so that they become self-reliant and self-sufficient. In fact, through the pursuit of sarvodaya ideals, Gandhi wanted to chart out an alternative course. The ideas on sarvodaya social order find their fullest expression in his constructive work programme that began to unfold itself on his arrival in India from South Africa. *Khadi*, communal amity, removal of untouchability, promotion of village industries, village sanitation, basic education, etc. came one after another and so did the supporting organization. Some of these organisations were: All India Spinners Association, All India Harijan Sewak Sangh, Hindustani Prachar Sabha, Hindustan Talimi Sangh and Akhil Bharat Sewa Sangh. The sarvodaya society is an ideal society and an ideal cannot be fully realized. Gandhi also believed that an ideal is never fully realized in life."[48]

Sarvodaya Political Order

Sarvodaya as a political doctrine is mildly anarchist. In fact, the political ideal of Sarvodaya is an anarchism of its own variety. It concedes that a fully stateless society is beyond the reach of man, and the goal of human endeavour can only be to reduce the power and sphere of the state to the minimum. The politics of sarvodaya is politics of *Lokniti* instead of *rajniti*. *Lokniti* is a comprehensive term, which denotes simultaneously a way of life a form of social order and a method. As a way of life, it stands for the self-regulation of individual conduct and for a habit to act on one's own initiatives. As a form of social order, it envisages a society in which police and military will have little to do and the law will interfere, least with life. A man will have the utmost freedom of action. As a method, it stands for social change in a manner that would maintain men's freedom of action.[49] The Sarvodaya Political Order is based on certain fundamental political assumptions:

(i) All individuals are equally born.

(ii) People are the custodians of the supreme power in the state.

(iii) Political power should be decentralized both at individual and the village level.

(iv) All must train themselves for self-rule.

(v) All should believe in the divinity of every individual and strive for the welfare of all people.[50]

The ultimate goal for Gandhi is the greatest good of all people. Good, to him, means only the self-realization but not the material well-being of the individuals or the society. A study on the nature of Sarvodaya Political Order demands a brief survey of his view on State, Swaraj, Satyagraha, Democracy, Nationalism, Internationalism and *Ram Rajya.*[51]

According to Vinoba Bhave[52], there are ten criteria of an ideal polity:

(i) International fraternity.

(ii) The conscious, spontaneous (as far as possible) and hearty co-operation of all the inhabitants of the country.

(iii) The identity of the good of the capable minority and the general majority.

(iv) The orientation towards the universal and equal development of all.

(v) The widest dispersion of political sovereignty.

(vi) The least amount of government.

(vii) The easiest availability of *tantra* or justice (?) – (*Sulabhatama tantra*).

(viii) The least possible expenditure.

(ix) The lowest degree of external protection.

(x) One universal, uninterrupted, and neutral or objective spread of knowledge.

Sarvodaya Economic Order

Gandhi adopted an integral approach to human problems. His basic aim was to reduce economics in terms of religion and spirituality. For him, ethics and economics are not two different entities. Economics that hurt the moral well-being of an individual or a nation are immoral and therefore sinful.[53] True economics, according to Gandhi "stands for social justice, it promotes the good of all equally including the weakest and is indispensable for decent life."[54] He mainly wants to formulate such an economic constitution to both India and the World that no one suffers from want of food, clothing and shelter. All necessities of life "should be freely available to all as God's air and water are or ought to be...".[55] Such an economic constitution, he aims at building not on material wealth but on spirituality. This is only possible when everyone shows more truth than gold, greater fearlessness than pomp of power and wealth, greater charity than love of self.

The Gandhian Sarvodaya economic order is based on simplicity, decentralization, self-sufficiency, co-operation, equality, non-violence, sanctity of labour, human values, self-sufficient village units, nationalization of basic industries, *swadeshi*, and the theory of trusteeship. These, in turn, will solve the problems pertaining to labour, capital, production, distribution and profit etc.

In the Gandhian Economic Order, dependence on others is slavery and self-sufficiency is freedom. Regional self-sufficiency is must in Sarvodaya Economic Order. People should produce their own needs of life. Production must be in accordance with the need.

In the Sarvodaya Economic Order, man is totally free from material bondage. He never becomes a slave to material wants. He lives above his greed and amassing of riches. He views work as service. It is divine for him. He cherishes the principles of self-suffering, sacrifice, dedication and renunciation. His eating, clothing or dwelling shows no superiority or inferiority. He finds no difference between the rich and the poor. Really Sarvodaya Economic System is practical, realistic and humane.

Socialism, Communism and Sarvodaya

Gandhi called himself a socialist and even a communist but for him socialism and communism were transcendental forms of egalitarian social philosophy that find their fulfilment and culmination in Sarvodaya.[56] Although the situational background from which Socialism and Sarvodaya have emerged is different, still their humanist idealism is almost similar.[57] According to Jayaprakash Narayan, Sarvodaya represents the highest socialist values. Socialism arose in the West as a philosophy of the industrial proletariat and challenged the pretensions of the contemporary state, which bolstered the interests of the capitalists.[58]

Socialism and Communism are basically idealistic, ethical and humanitarian in nature. They are concerned with the illumination of the misery of the millions, elevation of the status of poor, unfortunate and downtrodden and founding a society based on the principle of economic equality and social justice. Sarvodaya stands for the just society free from all types of exploitation and human miseries. According to Rajendra Prasad[59], Sarvodaya represents an aspiration "towards a society based on truth and non-violence in which there will be no distinction of caste or creed, no opportunity for exploitation and full scope for development both for individuals as well as groups." Jayaprakash Narayan[60] writes about Sarvodaya, "What we desire is the establishment of a society in which there will be no exploitation, there will be perfect equality and each individual will have equal opportunities for development."[61] Sarvodaya aims at a "classless, casteless and non-exploitative society."[62] Vinoba[63] said, "There is no permanent conflict between the two ideologies—Marxism and Sarvodaya. Whatever differences there might be between Gandhism and communism, there are also points of similarity between these and these too are important. The cause of the have-nots is the basic sentiment running through both. Both Gandhism and communism regard the well-being of the poor and the oppressed with the intensely loving regard of the Mother." K.G. Mashruwala, prominent

Gandhian observes, "the common point between Gandhi and Marx is the extreme concern of both for the suppressed and the oppressed, the resourceless and the ignorant, the dumb and starving section of humanity." Similarly, Jayaprakash Narayan[64] said, "If we are true socialists, we would be true follower of Sarvodaya as well."

In spite of some fundamental similarities between socialism and sarvodaya, there are great differences between them on the question of means and methods. From the sarvodaya stand point, there are two shortcomings in the socialist philosophy. First, the basic technique for effectuating socialism is supposed to be nationalization. But nationalization may entrench the control of the bureaucrats and may be another name for state capitalism. According to sarvodaya, the socialist belief in positive state action as the sovereign remedy for human ills is unfounded. Sarvodaya pleads for villagization while socialism believes in nationalization, sarvodaya accepts village ownership. Secondly, socialism adheres, at least in some cases, to the concept of violent revolution. But sarvodaya has no place for violence in its philosophy and technique.[65]

The differences between sarvodaya and communism are far more basic and fundamental. Communism advocates a violent technique for a change over in favour of egalitarian society, a society free from exploitation and privilege. Sarvodaya, to the contrary believes in persuasion and change of heart. Both Marx and Engels expressed their conviction that "violent overthrow of the bourgeoisie lays the foundation for the sway of the proletariat." Lenin and Mao used the technique of violence to bring about a change in the Soviet Union and China respectively. While Gandhi has taught the ethics of self-suffering to convert the opponent because violence can never be the foundation of a just and equal society.[66] Violence breeds counter-violence. And on the basis of violence it is not possible to establish the just social order. In fact, a new form of exploitation of man has come into existence and that is exploitation by the party bosses, bureaucrats and the state machinery.

The Sarvodaya avoids the evils of legislative or legal coercion in democratic socialism and violence and physical coercion involved in communism. It relies on the technique of conversion for bringing about social transformation in the direction of a non-exploitative and egalitarian society. Gandhi was concerned with the welfare of all and hence rejected the view that the welfare of all can ever be attained by physical, intellectual and moral coercion perpetrated by a section of the people against the rest of the community. Gandhi believed that sarvodaya could be realised only by the application of a moral and ethical method. Gandhi believed that through the application of the technique of persuasion and appeal to the innate good sense of the rich and the privileged, they might be made to renounce their privileges and apply their superfluous wealth for the welfare of the community. Such renunciation of wealth and privilege was to be for the good of the poor and the rich. "The essence of the revolution contemplated by sarvodaya is that it plans its faith on human approach, at the root of which stands the concept of revolution by human beings for the proliferation of human values and human virtues, and through a method that is strictly humane."[67]

The advocates of Sarvodaya also differ from the communists and socialists in respect of the role of the state. Both the communists and the socialists have their faith in the potency of the state to bring about equality in society. In the economic sphere, the communists and socialists advocate centralization and concentration of economic powers in the hands of the state and the proliferation of the economic activities of the state. To quote Jayaprakash Narayan[68]: "Democratic socialists, communists as well as welfarists are all statists." The concentration of both political and economic power in the hands of the state leads to too much of bureaucratisation, dehumanisation and loss of individual freedom. To quote Jayaprakash Narayan[69]: "The democratic state remains a Leviathan that will sit heavily on the freedom of the people." The state is still worse under communism. It is true that the communists talk about the withering away of the state in the long run, but during the transitional period, the state is not only tolerated but also becomes more and more powerful. It devours the lofty ideals of classless society—liberty, equality, fraternity and fellowship. Jayaprakash Narayan writes, "The remedy is to create and develop forms of socialist living through the voluntary endeavour of the people rather than seek to establish socialism by the use of the power of the state. In other words, the remedy is to establish people's socialism, rather than state socialism."[70]

Considering from all angles, Sarvodaya is a far nobler, subtler, loftier, broader, deeper and transcendental concept than socialism or communism. According to Vinoba, "Sarvodaya is a better word than 'socialist'; it is also our own native word, born from our own soil and carrying a noble meaning. We do not use the word because we are a little doubtful if we can live up to it. So we prefer the world 'socialist'. But our goal is in fact Sarvodaya and our people are being prepared for absorption into the sea of Sarvodaya." It is true that socialism and communism can realise their true meaning and fulfil their objective by merging their identity with sarvodaya. Jayaprakash Narayan[71] writes: "Socialism as we understand it today, cannot take mankind to the sublime goals of freedom, equality, brotherhood and peace. Socialism no doubt gives promise to bring mankind closer to those goals than any other competing social philosophy. But I am persuaded that unless socialism is transformed into sarvodaya, those goals would remain beyond its reach. Vinoba writes, "There is no permanent conflict between the two ideologies—Marxism and Sarvodaya. As the Ganges becomes wider and wider and moves on and finally merges in the ocean, I hope Marxism will merge in Sarvodaya one day."[72]

Sarvodaya and Contemporary Crisis

The Sarvodaya principles are capable of meeting the greatest challenge of the age. The most urgent need of today is the abolition of human suffering as well as of war. Even Sarvodaya will be very important in 21st Century due to complexity of human behaviour. Sarvodaya by laying stress on the goodness of human nature, unity of mankind, service of man, application of moral principles considered valid for individuals to group life and inter-state relations, the non-violent process of change, social and economic equality, economic and political decentralization, tries to resolve the various kinds of tensions that disturb domestic and international harmony. Sarvodaya is capable of strengthening the forces of love, creativeness and joy of life. Sarvodaya takes a whole view of man and emphasizes his spiritual nature. In modern context, the concept of Sarvodaya can be interpreted as the "awakening of one and all". Thus, in addition to the awakening of everyone, it refers to the awakening of the total human spirit and personality. Sarvodaya is also related to achieving the highest level of self-realization in which one sees one's manifestation in all others.

Our political, social and economic life has been sized with a malady. The malady of our times perhaps of all times, is mad quest for power, whether it is political, social or economic. Service is being given up in quest of personal aggrandisement. Humanity is undergoing almost a phase of moral collapse and ethical nihilism. In the era of the mad rush for power, the significance of Sarvodaya lies in stressing the permanent value of self-abnegation. Sarvodaya is giving expression to a moral principle of cardinal importance because it wants to enshrine the primacy of goodness and character in place of the skill of manipulation and self-assertion. Sarvodaya appeals to the mind and heart in terms of values and goals. The decadence and corruption, which in fact organized institutional mechanism, can be removed only by the reassertion of moral and spiritual values and their ever-growing incorporation in social, political and economic life. Sarvodaya is the only way to solve the problems of unemployment, unequal distribution of wealth, growing corruption in public life etc. The moral collapse and prostration of our world needs the revitalizing notion of ethical idealism and stress on the moral approach to social and economic problems, which Sarvodaya envisages.

Summing Up

Sarvodaya philosophy, based on the insights and experiences of Gandhi, is a reassertion of the valuation and moral approach to the problems of mankind, which has been a part of ancient Indian culture for ages. Vinoba Bhave rightly said "Sarvodaya stands for not only making all happy by illuminating suffering from all but also for bringing a world state based on equality."[73] For Gandhi, Sarvodaya stands for the merger of one in all with self-sacrifice and a selfless service. His Sarvodaya ideal, apart from standing for the meaning of the welfare of all, implies the meaning of the universal welfare and integrated development of all. As a universal ideal, it aims at not only fulfilling the minimum material needs but also developing the ethico-spiritual aspects of all people. The great contribution of Sarvodaya in the present century lies in the reassertion of the Gandhian moral approach to the problems of mankind and a vision that looks forward to the creation of a welfare state and society.

References

1. V. P. Verma, *The Political Philosophy of Mahatma Gandhi and Sarvodaya,* Lakshmi Naryan Agarwal, Agra, 1980, 4th Edition, p. 279.
2. J.N. Mohanty, "Sarvodaya and Aurobindo—a Rapprochement", *Gandhi Marg,* Vol. 4, No. 30, July 1960, p. 211.
3. B.P. Pandey, *Gandhi, Sarvodaya and Organizations,* Chugh Publications, Allahabad, 1988, pp. 20-21.
4. Vishwanath Tandon, *The Social and Political Philosophy of Sarvodaya After Gandhi,* Sarva Seva Sangh Prakashan, Varanasi, 1965, p. 2.
5. Anil Dutta Mishra, *Fundamentals of Gandhism,* Mittal Publications, New Delhi, 1995, p. 5.
6. Mahajan P. Mani and K.S. Bharathi, *Foundations of Gandhian Thought,* Dattsons, Nagpur, 1987, p. 68.
7. The Collected Works of Mahatama Gandhi, Vol. 8., Publications Division, Government of India, New Delhi, 1962, pp. 239-41.
8. K.M. Rathnam Chetty, *Sarvodaya and Freedom: A Gandhian Appraisal,* Discovery Publishing House, New Delhi, 1991, p. 46
9. B.S. Sharma, "The Philosophical Basis of Sarvodaya", *Gandhi Marg,* vol. 4, No. 3, July 1960, p. 259.
10. *Ibid.*
11. K.M. Rathnam Chetty, *op. cit.*, p. 47.
12. *Harijan*, 13.2.1949.
13. B.P. Pandey, *op. cit.*, p. 14.
14. Dada Dharmadhikari, *Sarvodaya Darshan,* Sarva Seva Sangh Prakashan, Varanasi, p. 18.
15. K.M. Rathnam Chetty, *op. cit.*, p. 48.
16. *Ibid.*, p. 38.
17. *Ibid.*
18. Benudhar Pradhan, *The Socialist Thought of Mahatma Gandhi,* G.D.K. Publications, Delhi, 1980, Vol. I, p. 284.
19. M.K. Gandhi, *An Autobiography: The Story of My Experiments with Truth,* Navjivan Publishing House, Ahmedabad, 1948, p. 365.

20. Benudhar Pradhan, *op. cit.*, p. 285.
21. K.M. Rathnam Chetty, *op. cit.*, pp. 39-40.
22. *Ibid.*, p. 40.
23. *Ibid.*, pp. 40-41.
24. *Ibid.*, p. 41.
25. *Ibid.*
26. M.K. Gandhi, *Young India*, 12-11-1925.
27. *Ibid.*
28. K.M. Rathnam Chetty, *op. cit.*, pp. 42-43.
29. Anil Dutta Mishra, *op. cit.*, p. 11.
30. *Ibid.*, p. 11.
31. Benudhar Pradhan, *op. cit.*, p. 294.
32. *Ibid.*, p. 301.
33. *Ibid.*, p. 302.
34. K.M. Rathnam Chetty, *op. cit.*, p. 45.
35. *Ibid.*
36. Jayaprakash Narayan, *Socialism, Sarvodaya and Communism*, A.P.H. Bombay, 1964, p. 149.
37. M.K. Gandhi, *Young India*, p. 364.
38. S. Gopalan, Means and Ends: The Gandhian View, *Gandhi Centenary Volume*, 1969, p. 70.
39. M.K. Gandhi, *Young India*, 17.7.1924.
40. D.G. Tendulkar, *Mahatma*, Vol. II, New Delhi, Publications Division, 1951, p. 299.
41. M.K. Gandhi, *Harijan*, 27.2.1949.
42. M.K. Gandhi, *Hind Swaraj or Indian Home Rule*, Ahmedabad, Navajivan Publishing House, 1946, p. 60.
43. *Harijan*, 27 February, 1949.
44. A.D. Mishra, *op. cit*, p. 14.
45. *Ibid.*
46. *Ibid.*, p. 15.

47. S.C. Gangal, *Gandhian Thought and Techniques in the Modern World*, Criterion Publications, New Delhi, 1988, pp. 158-59.
48. *Ibid.*, p. 159.
49. Vishwanath Tandon, *op. cit.*, pp. 124-25.
50. K.M. Rathnam Chetty, *op. cit.*, p. 66.
51. Anil Dutta Mishra, *op. cit.*, pp. 16-17.
52. V.P. Varma, *The Political Philosophy of Mahatma Gandhi and Sarvodaya*, Agra, Lakshmi Narayan Agarwal, 1980, p. 295.
53. N.K. Bose, *Selection From Gandhi*, Navjivan Publishing House, Ahmedabad, 1994, p. 40.
54. *Harijan*, 9 October, 1937.
55. *Young India*, 15 July, 1928.
56. V.D. Mahajan, *Modern Indian Political Thought*, p. 569.
57. Jayaprakash Narayan, *From Socialism to Sarvodaya,* Madras, Socialist Book Centre, 1956, p. 96.
58. V.P. Varma, *op. cit.*, p. 283.
59. V.D. Mahajan, *op. cit.*, p. 569.
60. *Ibid.*
61. *Ibid.*, pp. 569-70.
62. *Ibid.*, p. 570.
63. *Ibid.*
64. *Ibid.*
65. V.P. Varma, *op. cit.*, p. 285.
66. Vinoba Bhave, *Swarajya Shastra*, New Delhi, Sasta Sahitya Mandal, 1953, pp. 58-68.
67. V.D. Majahan, *op. cit.*, pp. 573-74.
68. Jayaprakash Narayan, *op. cit.*, p. 33.
69. *Ibid.*, p. 34.
70. *Ibid.*, p. 34.
71. *Ibid.*, p. 21
72. V.D. Mahajan, *op. cit.*, p. 574.
73. Anil Dutta Mishra, *op. cit.*, p. 17.

PART TWO
GANDHI ON SARVODAYA

2

Sarvodaya-I[1]

Preface

People in the West generally hold that it is man's duty to promote the happiness—prosperity, that is—of the greatest number.[2] Happiness is taken to mean material happiness exclusively, that is, economic prosperity. If, in the pursuit of this happiness moral, laws are violated, it does not matter much. Again, as the object is the happiness of the greatest number, people in the West do not believe it to be wrong if it is secured at the cost of the minority. The consequences of this attitude are in evidence in all western countries.

The exclusive quest for the physical and material happiness of the majority has no sanction in divine law. In fact, some thoughtful persons in the West have pointed out that it is contrary to divine law to pursue happiness in violation of moral principles. The late John Ruskin[3] was foremost among these. He was an Englishman of great learning. Hc has written numerous books on art and crafts. He has also written a great deal on ethical questions. One of these books, a small one, Ruskin himself believed to be his best. It is read widely wherever English is spoken. In the book, he has effectively countered these arguments and shown that the well-being of the people at large consists in conforming to the moral law.

We in India are much given now-a-days to imitation of the West. We do grant that it is necessary to imitate the West in certain respects. At the same time there is no doubt that many Western ideas are wrong. It will be admitted on all hands that what is bad must be eschewed. The condition of Indians in South Africa is pitiable. We go out to distant lands to make money. We are so taken up with this that we become oblivious of morality and of God. We become engrossed in the pursuit of self-interest. In the sequel, we find that going abroad does us more harm than good, or does not profit us as much as it ought to. All religions presuppose the moral law, but even if we disregard religion as such, its observance is necessary on grounds of common sense also. Our happiness consists in observing it. This is what John Ruskin has established. He has opened the eyes of the Western people to this, and today, we see a large number of Europeans modelling their conduct on his teaching. In order that Indians may profit by his ideas, we have decided to present extracts from his book, in a manner intelligible to Indians who do not know English.

Socrates gave us some idea of man's duty. He practised his precepts. It can be argued that Ruskin's ideas are an elaboration of Socratės. Ruskin has described vividly how one who wants to live by Socrates's ideas should acquit himself in the different vocations. The summary of his work which we offer here is not really a translation. If we translate it, the common reader might be unable to follow some of the Biblical allusions, etc. We present therefore, only the substance of Ruskin's work. We do not even explain what the title of the book means, for it be understood only by a person who has read the Bible in English.[4] But since the object which the book works towards is the welfare of all—that is, the advancement of all and not merely of the greatest number we have entitled these articles "Sarvodaya".

Roots of Truth[5]

Man suffers from many delusions; but none so great as his attempt to formulate laws for the conduct of other men disregarding the effects of social affection, as if they were only machines at work. That we cherish such an illusion does us no credit. Like other forms of error, the laws of political economy also contain an element of plausibility. Political economists assert that social affections are to be looked upon as accidental and disturbing elements in human nature; but avarice and the desire for progress are constant elements. Let us eliminate the inconstants and, considering man merely as a moneymaking machine, examine by what laws of labour, purchase and sale, the greatest amount of wealth can be accumulated. Those laws once determined, it will be for each individual afterwards to introduce as much of the disturbing affectional elements as he chooses.

This would be a convincing argument if the social affections were of the same nature as the laws of demand and supply. Man's affections constitute an inner force. The laws of demand and supply are formulations concerning the external world. The two, therefore, are not of the same nature. If a moving body is acted upon by a constant force from one direction and a varying force from another, we would first measure the constant force and then the inconstant. We will be able to determine the velocity of the body by comparing the two forces. We can do this because the constant and the inconstant forces are of the same kind. But in social dealings the constant force of the laws of demand and supply and the accidental force of social affection are forces that differ in kind. Affection has a different kind of effect on man and acts in a different manner. It changes man's nature, so that we cannot measure its effect with the help of laws of addition and subtraction, as we can the effects of different forces on the velocity of a body. A knowledge of the laws of exchange is of no help in determining the effects of man's social affections.

[From Gujarati]

— *Indian Opinion*, 16-5-1908

Notes

1. The Advancement of All.
2. The reference is to Bentham's maxim of "the greatest good of the greatest number". Gandhiji opposed it on moral grounds; *vide* "The Pietersburg Claptrap", 13-8-1904. Ruskin, too, criticized the construction of a "science" of economics on the Newtonain model from which "social affections" had been wholly abstracted. Ruskin argued that the greatest art or science was that which aroused "the greatest number of the greatest ideas".
3. *Vide* the parable of the Labourers in the Vineyard, *St. Matthew*, Ch. XX, *v.* 14. "I will give unto this last, even as unto thee."
4. (1819-1900); a Scotsman and author of many books on architecture, painting, social and industrial problems, the place of women in society, etc.; Slade Professor of Art in Oxford for some time; later became opposed to vivisection and usury and interested in workers' education and co-operative industrial settlements. Together with *Munera Pulveris*, *Unto This Last*, which was published as a series of articles in *Cornhill Magazine*, expounds Ruskin's social utopia. Gandhiji describes Ruskin as "one of the three moderns...who made a deep impress on me". *Unto This Last* "brought about an instantaneous and practical transformation....I arose with the dawn, ready to reduce these principles to practice". Polak commended this book to Gandhiji who read it on the train journey between Johannesburg and Durban. *Vide Autobiography*, Part IV, Ch. XVIII.
5. "Roots of Honour" in *Unto This Last*.

3

Sarvodaya-II

Roots of Truth

I do not doubt the conclusions of the science of economics [if its premises are accepted]. If a gymnast formulated laws on the assumption that man is made only of flesh without a skeleton, those laws might well be valid, but they would not apply to man, since man has a skeleton. In the same way, the laws of political economy may be valid but they cannot apply to man, who is subject to affections. A physical-culture expert may suggest that man's flesh be detached [from the skeleton], rolled into pellets, and then drawn out into cables.

He may then say that the re-insertion of the skeleton will cause little inconvenience. We should describe such a man as a madcap, for the laws of physical culture cannot be based on the separation of the skeleton from the flesh. In the same manner, the laws of political economy which exclude human affections are of no use to man. And yet the political economists of today behave exactly like the gymnastic instructor. According to their mode of reasoning, man is a mere body—a machine—and they base their laws on this assumption.

Though aware that man has a soul, they do not take it into account. How can such a science apply to man, in whom the soul is the predominant element? Every time there is a strike, we have a clean proof that economics is not a science, that it is worse than useless. In such situations, the employers take one view of the matter, the workers another. [Here] we cannot apply the laws of supply and demand. Men rack their brains to prove that the interests of the employers and the employees are identical. These men know nothing of such matters. In fact, it does not always follow that because their worldly interests—economic interests—are at variance men must be antagonistic to each other. Let us suppose that the members of a family are starving. The family consists of a mother and her children. They have only one crust of bread between them. All of them are hungry. Here, the interests of the two—of the mother on the one hand, and the children on the other—are mutually opposed. If the mother eats, the children will starve; if the children are fed, the mother will go hungry. There is no hostility between the mother and the children for that reason; they are not antagonistic to one another. Though the mother is the stronger, she does not eat up the bread. The same is true of men's relations with one another.

Let us suppose that there is no difference between men and animals, and that we must fight like animals in pursuit of our respective interests.[1] Even so we can lay down no general rule either way on whether or not the employer and the employee will always remain hostile to each other. Their attitudes change with circumstances. For instance, it is in the interest of both that work should be well and properly done and a just price obtained for it. But in the division of profits, the gain of the one may or may not be the loss of the other. It does not serve the employer's interests to pay wages so low as to leave his men sickly and depressed. Nor does it serve the worker's interests to demand a high wage irrespective of whether the factory pays its way or not. If the owner does not have enough money to keep the engine-wheels in repair, it will obviously be wrong for the worker to demand full wages or to demand any wages at all.

We can thus see that we are not likely to succeed in constructing a science on the basis of the principle of supply and demand. It was never God's intention that the affairs of men should be conducted on the principle of profit and loss. Justice must provide the basis. Man must give up, therefore, all thought of advancing his interests by following expediency regardless of moral considerations. It is not always possible to predict with certainty the outcome of a given line of conduct. But in most cases we can determine whether a certain act is just or unjust. We can also assert that the result of moral conduct is bound to be good. We cannot predict what that result will be, or how it will come about.

Justice includes affection. The relation between master and operative depends on this element of affection. Let us assume that the master wants to exact the utmost amount of work from his servant. He allows him no time for rest, pays him a low wage, and lodges him in a garret. In brief, he pays him a bare subsistence wage. It may be argued that there is no injustice in all this. The servant has placed all his time; at the master's disposal in return for a given wage, and the latter avails himself of it. He determines the limits of hardship in exacting work by reference to what others do. If the servant can get a better place, he is free to take it. This is called economics by those who formulate the laws of supply and demand. They assert that it is profitable to the master thus to exact the maximum amount of work for the minimum wage. In the long run, the entire society will benefit by it and, through the society, the servant himself.

But on reflection we find that this is not quite true. This method of calculation would have been valid if the employee were a mere machine which required some kind of force to drive it. But in this case, the motive power of the servant is his soul, and soul-force contradicts and falsifies all the calculations of the economists. The machine that is man cannot be driven by the money-fuel to do the maximum amount of work. Man will give of his best only when his affections are brought into play. The master-servant nexus must not be a pecuniary one, but one of love.

[From Gujarati]

— *Indian Opinion*, 23-5-1908

Note

1. The Gujarati has "common interests".

4

Sarvodaya-III

Roots of Truth

It usually happens that, if the master is a man of sense and energy, the servant works hard enough, under pressure; it also happens that, if the master is indolent and weak, the performance of the servant is not of the best in quality or quantity. But the true law is that, if we compare two masters of equal intelligence, the servant of the one who is sympathetically inclined will work better than that of the other who is not so inclined.

It may be argued that this principle does not quite hold, since kindness and indulgence are sometimes rewarded with their opposites.

The servant becomes unmanageable. But the argument is nevertheless invalid.

A servant who rewards kindness with negligence will become vengeful when treated harshly. A servant who is dishonest to a liberal master will be injurious to an unjust one.

Therefore, in any case and with any person, this unselfish treatment will yield the most effective return. We are here considering affections only as a motive power. That we should be kind because kindness is good is quite another consideration.

We are not thinking of that for the present. We only want to point out here that not only are the ordinary laws of economics, which we considered above, rendered nugatory by the motive power of kindness—sympathy—but also that affection, being a power of an altogether different kind, is inconsonant with the laws of economics and can survive only if those laws are ignored. If the master is a calculating person who shows kindness only in expectation of a return, he will probably be disappointed.

Kindness should be exercised for the sake of kindness; the reward will then come unsought. It is said that he who loses his life shall find it, and he who finds it shall lose it.[1]

Let us take the example of a regiment and its commander. If a general seeks to get his troops to work in accordance with the principles of economics, he will fail. There are many instances of generals cultivating direct, personal relations with their men, treating them with kindness, sharing their joys and hardships, ensuring their safety—in brief, treating them with sympathy. A general of this kind will be able to exact the most arduous work from his troops. If we look into history, we shall rarely find a battle won where the troops had no love for their general. Thus the bond of sympathy between the general and his troops is the truest force. Even a band of robbers has the utmost affection for its leader. And yet we find no such intimate relation between the employer and the employees in textile mills and other factories. One reason for this is that, in these factories, the wages of the employees are determined by the laws of supply and demand.

Between the employer and the employee there obtains, therefore, the relation of disaffection rather than of affection, and instead of sympathy between them we find antagonism. We have then to consider two questions: one, how far the rate of wages may be so regulated as not to vary with the demand for labour; second, how far workmen can be maintained in factories, without any change in their numbers irrespective of the state of trade, with the same bond [between workmen and employer] as obtains between servants and master in an old family, or between soldiers and their commander.

Let us consider the first question. It is surprising why economists do nothing to make it possible for standards of payment for factory workers to be fixed. We see, on the other hand, that the office of the Prime Minister of England is not put up to auction, but that whoever the incumbent, the remuneration remains the same. Nor do we offer the job of a priest to anyone who agrees to accept the lowest salary. With physicians and lawyers, too, we do not generally deal in this manner. Thus, we observe that in these instances a certain standard of payment is fixed. It may be asked, however, whether a good workman and a bad one must both be paid the same wage. In fact, that is as it should be. In the result, the rate of wages for all workers being the same, we shall engage only a good bricklayer or carpenter as we go only to a good physician or lawyer—the fees of all physicians or lawyers being the same. That is the proper reward of the good workman— to be chosen. Therefore, the right system respecting all labour is that it should be paid at fixed rates. Where a bad workman finds it possible to deceive employers by accepting a low wage, the eventual outcome cannot but be bad.

Let us now consider the second point. It is that, whatever the state of trade, the factories must maintain the same number of workers in employment. When there is no security of employment, the workers are obliged to ask for higher wages. If, however, they can be assured of continued employment for life, they will be prepared to work for very low wages. It is clear, therefore, that the employer who assures security of employment to his workers will find it profitable in the long run. The employees also stand to gain, if they continue steadily in the same job. Large profits are not possible in factories run on these lines.

Big risks cannot be taken. Gambling on a large scale will not be possible. The soldier is ready to lay down his life for the sake of his commander. That is why the work of a soldier is considered more honourable than that of an ordinary worker. The soldier's trade is really, not slaying, but being slain in defence of others. Anyone who enlists as a soldier holds his life at the service of the state. This is true also of the lawyer, the physician and the priest. That is why we look up to them with respect. A lawyer must do justice even at the cost of his life. The physician must treat his patients at the cost of inconvenience to himself. And the clergyman must instruct his congregation and direct it along the right path, regardless of consequences.

[From Gujarati]

—*Indian Opinion,* 30-5-1908

Note

1. *St. Matthew,* Ch. X, *v.* 39.

5

Sarvodaya-IV

Roots of Truth

If this can happen in the professions mentioned, why not in trade and commerce? Why is it that trade is always associated with unscrupulousness? We shall see on reflection that it is always assumed that the merchant is moved [solely] by self-interest. Even though he has a socially useful function, we take it for granted that his object is to fill his own coffers. Even the laws are so drafted as to enable the merchant to amass wealth with the utmost speed. It is also accepted as a principle that the buyer must offer the lowest possible price and the seller must demand and accept the highest. The trader has thus been encouraged in this habit, yet the public themselves look down on him for his dishonesty. This principle must be abandoned. It is not right that the merchant should look only to self-interest and amass wealth. This is not trade, but robbery. The soldier lays down his life for the state and the trader ought to suffer [a comparable] loss, ought even to lose his life in the interests of society. In all states the soldier's profession is to defend the people; the pastor's to teach it; the physician's to keep it in health; the lawyer's to enforce pure justice in it; and the merchant's to provide for it. And it is the duty of each on due occasion to die for the people. The soldier must be prepared to die at his post of duty rather than desert it. During a plague epidemic, the physician must not run away [from his task] but instead attend to the patients even at the risk of infection. The priest must lead people from error to truth even if they should kill him for it. The lawyer must ensure, even at the cost of his life, that justice prevails.[1]

We pointed out above the proper occasions for members of the professions to lay down their lives. What, then, is the proper occasion for the merchant to lay down his life? This is a question which all, the merchant included, must ask themselves. The man who does not know when to die does not know how to live. We have seen that the merchant's function is to provide for the people. Just as the clergyman's function is not to earn a stipend but to instruct, so the merchant's function is not to make profits but to provide for the people. The clergyman who devotes himself to preaching has his needs provided for, and in the same manner the merchant will have his profits. But neither of them must have an eye only on the main chance. Both have work to do—each a duty to perform—irrespective of whether or not they get the stipend or the profit. If this proposition is true, the merchant deserves the highest honour. For his duty is to procure commodities of high quality and distribute them at a price which people can afford. It also becomes his duty at the same time to ensure the safety and well-being of the hundreds or thousands of men working under him. This requires a great deal of patience, kindness and intelligence.

Also, in discharging these several functions he is bound, as others are bound, to give up his life, if need be. Such a trader would not sell adulterated goods or cheat anyone, whatever his difficulties or even if he was going to be reduced to utter poverty. Moreover, he will treat the men under him with the utmost kindness. Very often a young man taking up a situation with a big factory or commercial house travels a long way from home, so that the master has to accept the role of his parents. If the master is indifferent, the young man will be like an orphan. At every step, therefore, the merchant or the master must ask himself this question, 'Do I deal with my servants as I do with my sons?'

Suppose a ship's captain places his son among the common sailors under his command. The captain's duty is to treat all sailors as he would treat his son. In the same manner, a merchant may ask his son to work alongside of those under him. He must always treat the workers as he would then treat his son. This is the true meaning of economics. And as the captain is bound to be the last man to leave his ship in case of shipwreck, so in the event of famine or other calamities, the trader is bound to safeguard the interests of his men before his own. All this may sound strange. But the really strange thing about the modern age is that it should so sound. For anyone who applies his mind to it will be able to see that the true principle is as we have stated it. Any other standard is impossible for a progressive nation. If the British have survived so long, it is not because they have lived up to the maxims of economics, but because they have had many heroes who have questioned them and followed instead these principles of moral conduct. The harm that results from the violation of these principles and the nation's consequent decline from greatness, we shall consider on another occasion.

[From Gujarati]

— *Indian Opinion*, 6-6-1908

Note

1. Ruskin found Beauty in "the appearance of felicitous fulfilment of function in living things, more especially of the joyful and right exertion of perfect life in man" (*Modern Painters*, Vol. II, Part III, Sec. I, Ch. 3.). Gandhiji, too, speaks of the beauty of *satyagraha*, which is "suffering undergone to exemplify Truth". To see Truth is to assent to it, and thus it helps Reason as a means of ordering social relations.

6

Sarvodaya-V

Veins of Wealth

Economists may reply in the following manner to what we said earlier concerning "roots of truth": 'It is true that certain advantages flow from social affection. But economists do not take these advantages into their reckoning. The science with which they are concerned is the science of getting rich. Far from being fallacious, it has in experience been found to be effective. Those who follow it do become rich, and those who disregard it become poor. All the millionaires of Europe have acquired their wealth by following the laws of this science. It is futile to seek to controvert this. Everyman of the world knows how money is made and how it is lost.'

This is not quite true. Men of business do indeed make money but they do not know whether they make it by fair means and if their money-making contributes to the national weal. Very often they do not even know the meaning of the word "rich". They do not realize that, if there are rich men, there must also be poor men. People sometimes believe, mistakenly, that by following certain precepts it is possible for everybody to become rich. But the true position can be compared to a water-wheel where one [bucket] empties out as another fills. The power of the rupee you possess depends on another going without it. If no one wants it, it will be useless to you. The power it possesses depends on your neighbour's lack of it. There can be wealth only where there is scarcity. This means that, in order to be rich, one must keep another poor.

Political economy consists in the production, preservation and distribution, at the fittest time and place, of useful and pleasurable things. The farmer who reaps his harvest at the right time, the builder who lays bricks properly, the carpenter who attends to woodwork with care, the woman who runs her kitchen efficiently are all true political economists. All of them add to the national income. A science that teaches the opposite of this is not "political". Its only concern is with individuals merely accumulating a certain metal and putting it to profitable use by keeping others in want of it. Those who do this estimate their wealth—the value of their farms and cattle—by the number of rupees they can get for them, rather than the value of their rupees by the number of cattle and farms they can buy with them.

Furthermore, men who thus accumulate metal—rupees—think [in terms] of the number of workmen whose services they can command.

Let us suppose that a certain individual possesses gold, silver, corn, etc.

This person will require a servant. And, if none of his neighbours is in need of gold, silver or corn, he will find it difficult to get one. He will then have to bake his bread, make his clothes and plough his field all by himself. This man will find his gold to be of no greater value than the yellow pebbles on his estate. His hoard of corn will rot. For he cannot consume more than his neighbour. He must, therefore, maintain himself by hard labour as other men do. Most people will not want to accumulate gold or silver on these terms. Careful reflection will show that what we really desire through acquisition of wealth is power over other men—[power] to acquire for our advantage the labour of a servant, a tradesman or an artisan. And the power we can thus acquire will be in direct proportion to the poverty of others. If there is only one person [in a position] to employ a carpenter, the latter will accept whatever wage is offered. If there are three or four persons who need his services, he will work for the person who offers him the highest wage. So that growing rich means contriving that as large a number of men as possible shall have less than we have. Economists generally assume that it is of advantage to the nation as a whole if the mass of people are thus kept in want. Equality among men is certainly not possible. But conditions of scarcity, unjustly created, injure the nation.

Scarcity and abundance arising naturally make, and keep, the nation happy.

[From Gujarati]

— *Indian Opinion,* 13-6-1908

7
Sarvodaya-VI

Veins of Wealth

Thus, the circulation of wealth among people resembles the circulation of blood in the body. When circulation of blood is rapid, it may indicate any of these things: robust health, [effects of] exercise, or a feeling of shame or fever. There is a flush of the body which is indicative of health, and another which is a sign of gangrene. Furthermore, the concentration of blood at one spot is harmful to the body and, similarly, concentration of wealth at one place proves to be the nation's undoing.

Let us suppose that two sailors are shipwrecked on an uninhabited coast. They are then obliged to produce food and other necessaries of life through their own labour. If they both keep good health and work in amity, they may build a good house, till the land and lay by something for the future. All these things would constitute real wealth. If both of them work equally well they will have equal shares. Therefore, all that [economic] science would have to say about their case is that they had acquired a right to an equal share in the fruits of their labour. Let us suppose now that after a while one of them feels discontented. So they divide the land and each one works on his land by himself and on his own account. Let us suppose that at a critical time one of them falls ill. He would then approach the other for help. The latter might reply: 'I shall do this work for you, but on condition that you do the same amount of work for me when required. You must undertake in writing to work on my field when required for the same number of hours that I work [for you now].'

Suppose further that the disabled man's illness continues and that everytime he has to give a written promise to the other, healthy person. What will be the position of the reduced to utter poverty? For, during the time that the invalid was laid up, his labour was unavailable.

Even assuming that the friend was very hard-working, it is obvious that the time which he devoted to the ailing man's land was at the expense of work on his own. This means that the combined property of the two would be less than it would have been otherwise.

Also, the relation in which the two stood to each other has altered. The sick man becomes a debtor, and can only offer his labour [as payment towards the debt]. Suppose now that the healthy man decided to make use of the documents in his possession. He would then find it possible wholly to abstain, from work—that is, be idle. If he chose, he could exact further pledges[1] from the man who has recovered. No one can attribute any illegality to such a transaction. If now a stranger was to arrive on the scene, he would find that one of the two men had become wealthy and the other had lost his well-being. He would also see one of them passing his days in idle luxury and the other in want, though labouring hard. The reader will note from this that claiming the fruits of another's labour as of right.

Let us consider another illustration. [Suppose that] three men established a kingdom[2] and then they all lived separately. Each of them raised a different crop which the others could also avail themselves of. Suppose, further, that one of them, in order to save the time of all the three, gave up farming and undertook to arrange the transfer of commodities from one to the other, receiving in return a quantity of foodgrains. If this man provided the [required] commodity[3] at the right time, all of them would prosper. Now suppose that he kept back some of the grain he was to transfer. Then suppose there set in a period of scarcity, and the middleman offered the stolen corn at an exorbitant price. In this way he could reduce both the farmers to poverty and employ them as labourers.

This would be a case of obvious injustice. This is, however, the way the merchants of today manage their affairs. We can also see that in consequence of this fraudulent practice the wealth of the three, taken collectively, will be less than it would have been if the [middle]man had behaved honestly. The other two farmers have done less work [than they could have]. Because they could not obtain the supplies they wanted, their labour did not fructify to the fullest, and the stolen commodities[4] the hands of the dishonest middleman were not put to the most effective use.

We can, therefore, reckon with mathematical accuracy how far the estimate of a nation's wealth depends on the manner in which that wealth has been acquired. We cannot estimate a nation's wealth on the basis of the quantity of cash it possesses. Cash in the hands of an individual may be a token of perseverance, skill and prosperity, or of harmful luxuries, merciless tyranny and chicanery. Our way of estimating wealth not only takes into account the moral attributes [of the different modes of acquiring it] but is also sound mathematically. One stock of money is such that it has created ten times as much in the gathering of it. Another is such that it has annihilated ten times as much in the gathering of it.

To lay down directions for the making of money without regard to moral considerations is, therefore, a pursuit that bespeaks of man's insolence. There is nothing more disgraceful to man than the principle "buy in the cheapest market and sell in the dearest". Buy in the cheapest market? Yes, but what made your market cheap? Charcoal may be cheap among roof timbers after a fire and the bricks of buildings brought down by an earthquake may be cheap. But no one, therefore, will make bold to assert that fire and earthquake redound to the nation's benefit. Again, sell in the dearest market? Yes, but what made your market dear? You made good profit today from the sale of your bread. But was it by extorting the last cowrie from a dying man?

Or, did you sell it to a rich man who will tomorrow appropriate all that you have? Or did you give it to a bandit on his way to pillaging your bank? Probably, you will not be able to answer any of these questions, for you do not know. But there is one question you can answer, namely, whether you sold it justly and at a reasonable price? And justice is all that matters. It is your duty to act so that no one suffers through your actions.

[From Gujarati]

— *Indian Opinion,* 20-6-1908

Notes

1. Pledges of bonded labour in return for the provision of the debtor's current needs leads to a diminution of real wealth.
2. "Republic" in *Unto This Last.*
3. Farming implements, seeds, etc.
4. The foodgrains and farming implements withheld by the middleman.

8

Sarvodaya-VII

Veins of Wealth

We saw that the value of money consists in its power to command the labour of men. If that labour could be had without payment, there should be no further need of money. Instances are known where human labour can be had without payment. We have considered examples which show that moral power is more effective than the power of money. We also saw that man's goodness can do what money cannot do. There exist men in many parts of England who cannot be beguiled with money.

Moreover, if we admit that wealth carries with it the power to direct labour, we shall also see that the more intelligent and moral men are, the greater is the wealth amassed. It may even appear on a fuller consideration that the persons themselves constitute the wealth, not gold and silver. We must search for wealth not in the bowels of the earth, but in the hearts of men. If this is correct, the true law of economics is that men must be maintained in the best possible health, both of body and mind, and in the highest state of honour. A time may also come when England, instead of adorning the turbans of its slaves with diamonds from Golkonda and thus sporting her wealth, may be able to point to her great men of virtue, saying, in the words of a truly eminent Greek, "This is my wealth."

Even-Handed Justice[1]

Some centuries before Christ there lived a Jewish merchant, Solomon[2] name. He had made a large fortune and earned great fame.

His maxims are remembered in Europe even today. He was so beloved of the Venetians that they erected a statue in the city to his memory.

Though his maxims are known by rote, very few persons actually practise them. He says: "Those who make money through lies are afflicted with pride, and that is a sign of their death." At another place, he adds: "Treasures of wickedness profit nothing. It is truth which delivers from death."[3] In both these maxims Solomon asserts that death is the outcome of wealth unjustly acquired. Now-a-days, people tell lies or perpetrate injustice so cleverly that we cannot find them out. For there are misleading advertisements. Things bear attractive labels, and so on.

Again the wise man says: "He that oppresseth the poor to multiply his riches shall surely come to want." And he adds: "Rob not the poor because he is poor. Oppress not the afflicted in the place of business. For God[4] will corrupt the soul of those that torment them." At present, however, it is the practice in business to administer kicks to those who are already dead. We are eager to take advantagc of a needy man. The highwayman robs the rich, but the trader robs the poor.

Solomon says further: "The rich and the poor are equal. God is their maker. God gives them knowledge."[5] The rich and the poor cannot live, the one without the other. They always need each other. Neither of them can be regarded as superior or inferior to the other. But evil consequences follow when the two forget that they are equal, and that God is their light.

[From Gujarati]

— *Indian Opinion*, 27-6-1908

Notes

1. This corresponds to Ruskin's chapter "*Qui Judicatis Terram*". "Ye that be judges of the earth, [love righteousness]."
2. (993-953 B.C.); believed in Ruskin's day to have been the author of *Proverbs* in the Old Testament.
3. Cf. *Proverbs,* Ch. XXI, *v.* 6 and Ch. X, *v.* 2.
4. The Gujarati has "Khuda".
5. Cf. *Proverbs*, Ch. XXII, *v.* 2: "The rich and poor meet together: the Lord is the maker of them all" and *Proverbs,* Ch. XXIX, *v.* 13: "The poor and the deceitful man meet together: the Lord lighteneth both their eyes." Ruskin himself used the Vulgate.

9

Sarvodaya-VIII

Wealth is like a river. A river always flows towards the sea, that is, down an incline. So, as a general rule must wealth go where it is needed. But the flow of wealth, like the course of a river, can be regulated. Most of the rivers run out their courses unregulated, their marshy banks poisoning the wind. If dams are built across these rivers to direct the water flow as required, they will irrigate the soil and keep the atmosphere pure. Similarly, the uncontrolled use of wealth will multiply vices among men and cause starvation; in brief, such wealth will act like a poison. But the selfsame wealth, if its circulation is regulated and its use controlled, can, like a river whose stream has been properly harnessed, promote prosperity.

The principle of regulating the circulation of wealth is ignored altogether by economists. Theirs is merely the science of getting rich.

But there are many different ways of getting rich. There was a time in Europe when people sought to acquire wealth by poisoning owners of large estates and appropriating their possessions. Now-a-days, merchants adulterate the food sold to the poor, for example, milk with borax, [wheat] flour with potato flour, coffee with chicory, butter with fat and so on. This is on the same level as getting rich by poisoning others. Can we call this either an art or a science of getting rich?

Let us not, however, assume that by "getting rich" economists merely mean "getting rich by robbing others". They should point out that theirs is a science of getting rich by legal or just means. It happens these days that many things which are legal are not just. The only right way, therefore, to acquire wealth is to do so justly. And, if this is true, we must know what is just. It is not enough to live by the laws of demand and supply. Fish, wolves and rats subsist in that manner. Bigger fish prey on smaller ones, rats swallow insects and wolves devour even human beings. That for them is the law [of Nature]; they know no better. But God has endowed man with understanding, with a sense of justice. He must follow these and not think of growing rich by devouring others—by cheating others and reducing them to beggary.

Let us examine what then the laws of justice regarding payment of labour are.

As we stated earlier, a just wage for a worker will be that which will secure him the same labour, when he needs it, as he has put in for us today. If we give him a lower wage, he will be underpaid, and if more, overpaid.

[Suppose] a man wants to engage a worker. Two persons offer their services. If the man who offers to accept a lower wage is engaged, he will be underpaid. If there is a large number of employers and only one worker, he will get his own terms and will very likely be overpaid. The just wage lies between these two points.

If someone lends me money which I have to repay after a time, I shall pay him interest. Similarly, if someone gives me his labour today, I must return him an identical quantity of labour and something more by way of interest. If someone gives me an hour [of labour] today, I should promise to give him an hour and five minutes or more. This is true of every kind of worker.

If, now, of two men who offer me their services, I engage the one who accepts the lower wage, the result will be that he will be half starved while the other man will remain unemployed. Even otherwise, if I pay full wages to the workman whom I employ, the other man will be unemployed. But the former will not starve, and I shall have made just use of my money. Starvation really occurs only when the due wages are not paid. If I pay due wages, surplus wealth will not accumulate in my hands. I shall not waste money on luxuries and add to the poverty. The workman whom I pay justly will in turn learn to pay others justly. Thus, the stream of justice will not dry up; instead it will gather speed as it flows. And the nation which has such a sense of justice will grow happy and prosper in the right direction.

According to this line of reasoning, economists are found to be wrong. They argue that increased competition means growing prosperity for a nation. This is not true in fact. Competition is desired because it reduces the rate of wages. The rich become richer thereby and the poor poorer. Such competition is likely to ruin a nation in the long run. The right law of demand and supply should ensure the payment of a just wage to a workman according to his worth. This, too, will mean competition, but the result will be that people will be happy and skilful, for, instead of being obliged to underbid one another, they will have to acquire [new] skills to secure employment.

It is for this reason that men are drawn to government service. There, salaries are fixed according to the gradation of posts. The competition is only with regard to ability. A candidate does not offer to accept a lower salary but claims that he is abler than others. The same is the case with the Army and the Navy, and that is why there is much less corruption in these services. But only in trade and commerce is there unhealthy competition, as a result of which corrupt practices, such as fraud, chicanery, theft, have increased. Furthermore, goods of poor quality are manufactured. The manufacturer wants a lion's share [of the price] for himself, the workman to throw dust in the eyes of others and the consumer to exploit the situation to his own advantage.

This poisons all human intercourse, there is starvation all round, strikes multiply, manufacturers become rogues and consumers disregard ethical considerations. One injustice leads to numerous others, and in the end the employer, the operative and the customer are all unhappy and meet with ruin. A people among whom these [corrupt] practices prevail comes to grief in the end. Its very wealth acts like a poison.

This is why men of wisdom have held that where Mammon is God, no one worships the true God. Wealth cannot be reconciled with God. God lives only in the homes of the poor. This is what the British profess, but in practice they place wealth above everything else, estimate the prosperity of the nation by the number of its rich, and their economists formulate precepts for everyone to get rich quickly.

True economics is the economics of justice. That people alone will be happy which learns how to do justice and be righteous under all conditions of life. All else is vain, a kind of moral perversity that presages doom. To teach the people to get rich at any cost is to teach them an evil lesson.

[From Gujarati]

— *Indian Opinion*, 4-7-1908

10

Sarvodaya-IX

What is Just?

We saw in the three preceding chapters that the generally accepted principles of economics are invalid. If acted upon, they will make individuals and nations unhappy. The poor will become poorer and the rich richer; neither will be any the happier for it.

Economists do not take men's conduct into account but estimate prosperity from the amount of wealth accumulated and so conclude that the happiness of nations depends upon their wealth alone. Hence, they advocate greater accumulation of wealth through more and more work in factories. In England and elsewhere, factories have multiplied because of the spread of these ideas. Large numbers of men leave their farms and concentrate in cities. They give up the pure and fresh air of the countryside and feel happy breathing the foul air of factories. As a result, the nation grows weaker, and avarice and immorality increase, and if someone suggests measures for eradicating vice, the so-called wise men argue that vice cannot be eliminated, that the ignorant cannot be educated all at once and that it is best to let things alone. While advancing this argument, they forget that it is the rich who are responsible for the immorality of the poor.

The wretched workers slave for them day and night so that they may be kept supplied with their luxuries. They have not a moment to themselves for self-improvement. Thinking about the rich, they also want to be rich. When they fail in this, they become angry and resentful. They then forget themselves [in their anger], and having failed to gather wealth by honest means, turn in desperation to fraud.

Both wealth and labour are thus wasted, else they are utilized for promoting fraud.

Labour, in the real sense of the term, is that which produces useful articles. Useful articles are those which support human life. Supporting human life means provision of food, clothing, etc., so as to enable men to live a moral life and to do good while they live. For this purpose, large-scale industrial undertakings would appear to be useless.

To seek to acquire wealth by establishing big factories is likely to lead to sin. Many people amass wealth but few make good use of it. If the making of money is likely to lead a nation to its destruction, that money is useless. On the contrary, present-day capitalists are responsible for widespread and unjust wars. Most of the wars of our times spring from greed for money.

We hear people say that it is impossible to educate others so as to improve them, and the best course would be to live as well as one could and accumulate wealth. Those who hold these views show little concern for ethical principles. For the person who values ethical principles and does not yield to avarice has a disciplined mind; he does not stray from the right path, and influences others merely by his example.

If the individuals who constitute a nation do not observe moral principles of conduct how can the nation become moral? If we behave as we choose and then point the accusing finger at an errant neighbour, how can the result [of our actions] be good?

We thus see that money no more than a means which may make for happiness or misery. In the hands of a good man, it can be used for cultivating land and raising crops. Cultivators will find contentment in innocent labour and the nation will be happy. In the hands of bad men, it is used for the production, say, of gunpowder and bringing utter ruin on the people. Both those who manufacture gunpowder and those who fall victims to it suffer in consequence. We thus see that there is no wealth besides life. That nation is wealthy which is moral. This, not the time for self-indulgence. Everyone must work according to his ability. As we saw in the illustrations earlier, if one man remains idle another has to labour twice as hard.[1] This is at the root of the starvation prevalent in England. There are men who do little useful work themselves because of the wealth that has accumulated in their hands, and so force others to labour for them. This kind of labour, being unproductive, is not beneficial to the worker. In consequence, the income suffers diminution. Though all men appear to be employed, we find on closer scrutiny that a large number are idle perforce. Moreover, envy is aroused, discontent takes root and, in the end, the rich and the poor, the employer and the workman violate the bounds of decency [in their mutual relations]. As the cat and the mouse are always at variance with each other, so the rich and the poor, the employer and the workman become hostile to one another, and man, ceasing to be man, is reduced to the level of beasts.

Conclusion

Our summary of the great Ruskin's book is now concluded.

Though some may have been bored by it, we advise those who have read the articles once to read them again. It will be too much to expect that all the readers of *Indian Opinion* will ponder over them and act on them. But even if law readers make a careful study of the summary and grasp the central idea, we shall deem our labour to have been amply rewarded. Even if that does not happen, the reward [of labour], as Ruskin says in the last chapter, consists in having done one's duty and that should satisfy one.

What Ruskin wrote for his countrymen, the British, is a thousand times more applicable to Indians. New ideas are spreading in India.

The advent of a new spirit among the young who have received Western education is, of course, to be welcomed. But the outcome will be beneficial only if that spirit is canalized properly; if it is not, it is bound to be harmful. From one side we hear the cry for *swarajya*; from another, for the quick accumulation of wealth by setting up factories like those in Britain.

Our people hardly understand what *swarajya* means. Natal enjoys *swarajya*, but we would say that, if we were to imitate Natal, *swarajya* would be no better than hell. [The Natal whites] tyrannize over the Kaffirs, hound out the Indians, and in their blindness give free rein to selfishness. If, by chance, Kaffirs and Indians were to leave Natal, they would destroy themselves in a civil war.

Shall we, then, hanker after the kind of *swarajya* which obtains in the Transvaal? General Smuts is one of their leading figures. He does not keep any promise, oral or written. He says one thing, does another. The British are disgusted with him. Under the guise of effecting economy, he has deprived British soldiers of livelihood and has been replacing them with Dutchmen. We do not believe that in the long run this will make even the Dutch happy. Those who serve only their own interests will be ready to rob their own-people after they have done with robbing others.

If we observe happenings all over the world, we shall be able to see that what people call *swarajya* is not enough [to secure] the nation's prosperity and happiness. We can perceive this by means of a simple example. All of us can visualize what would happen if a band of robbers were to enjoy *swarajya.* In the long run they would be happy only if they were placed under the control of men who were not themselves robbers. America, France and England are all great States. But there is no reason to think that they are really happy.

Real *swarajya* consists in restraint. He alone is capable of this who leads a moral life, does not cheat anyone, does not forsake truth and does his duty to his parents, his wife, his children, his servant and his neighbour. Such a man will enjoy *swarajya* wherever he may happen to live. A nation that has many such men always enjoys *swarajya.*

It is wrong normally for one nation to rule over another. British rule in India is an evil but we need not believe that any very great advantage would accrue to the Indians if the British were to leave India. The reason why they rule over us is to be found in ourselves; that reason is our disunity, our immorality and our ignorance.[2]

If these three things were to disappear, not only would the British leave India without the rustling of a leaf, but it would be real *swarajya* that we would enjoy.

Many people exult at the explosion of bombs.[3] This only shows ignorance and lack of understanding. If all the British were to be killed, those who kill them would become the masters of India, and as a result India would continue in a state of slavery. The bombs with which the British will have been killed will fall on India after the British leave. The man who killed the President of the French Republic was himself a Frenchman and the assassin of President Cleveland of America was an

American.[4] We ought to be careful, therefore, not to be hasty and thoughtlessly to imitate the people of the West.

Just as we cannot achieve real *swarajya*, by following the path of evil—that is by killing the British—so also will it not be possible for us to achieve it by establishing big factories in India. Accumulation of gold and silver will not bring *swarajya.* This has been convincingly proved by Ruskin.

Let it be remembered that Western civilization is only a hundred years old, or to be more precise, fifty. Within this short span, the Western people appear to have been reduced to a state of cultural anarchy. We pray that India may never be reduced to the same state as Europe. The Western Nations are impatient to fall upon one another, and are restrained only by the accumulation of armaments all-round.

When [the situation] flares up, we will witness a veritable hell let loose in Europe. All [white] nations look upon the black races as their legitimate prey. This is inevitable when money is the only thing that matters. Wherever they find any territory, they swoop down on it like crows upon carrion. There are reasons to suggest that this is the outcome of their large industrial undertakings.

To conclude, the demand of *swarajya* is the demand of every Indian, and it is a just demand. But *swarajya* is to be achieved by righteous means. It must be real *swarajya.* It cannot be achieved by violent methods or by setting up factories. We must have industry, but of the right kind. India was once looked upon as a golden land, because Indians then were people of sterling worth. The land is still the same but the people have changed and that is why it has become arid. To transform it into a golden land again we must transmute ourselves into gold by leading a life of virtue. The philosophers' stone which can bring this about consists of two syllables: *satya.* If, therefore, every Indian makes it a point to follow truth always, India will achieve *swarajya* as a matter of course.

This is the substance of Ruskin's book.

[From Gujarati]

— *Indian Opinion*, 18-7-1908

Notes

1. *Vide* "Sarvodaya [VI]", 20-6-1908.
2. *Vide* "The Deputation's Voyage-II", 11-10-1906.
3. Gandhiji may have been thinking of the Muzaffarpur bomb incident; *vide* "Turmoil in India", 9-5-1908.
4. President Cleveland died a natural death. Gandhiji may have had Lincoln in mind; *vide* "Abraham Lincoln", 26-8-1905.

Glossary

Ahimsa	Non-violence
Anasakti	Non-attachment
Aparigraha	Non-possession
Ashram	Hermitage; Stages of life—Brahmacharya, Grihastha, Banaprashtha and Sanaysi
Aashramite	Inmate of ashram
Bhakti	Devotion
Brahmacharya	Celibacy
Charkha	Spinning wheel
Daridranarayan	God embodied as the poor
Dharma	Duty; one of the four purusharthas—Dharma, Artha, Kama and Moksha
Gram	Village
Guru	Spritual teacher
Harijans	People of God (the name used by Gandhiji for people of the caste of "untouchables")
Hartal	Strike
Kanchan	Gold
Kama	Sexual desire
Kamini	Women
Karma	Action
Karma	The ethical law of causation
Khadi	Hand-spun cloth
Moksha	Salvation, release from the cycle of rebirth; one of the four purusharthas—Dharma, Artha, Kama and Moksha

Poorna Swaraj	Complete Independence
Praja	People
Ramayana	A Hindu epic
Ramrajya	The rule of Ram, the rule of God
Satyagraha	Truth force; Insistence on Truth
Satyagrahi	Non-violent resister
Smriti	Oral Knowledge
Swadeshi	Insistence on local products
Swaraj	Self Rule, Home Rule, Self-government
Tapasya	The practice of austerities
Upanishads	Hindu sacred texts which form the final part of the Vedas
Varna	Caste
Varnashrama	Four fold division in Hindu society

Index